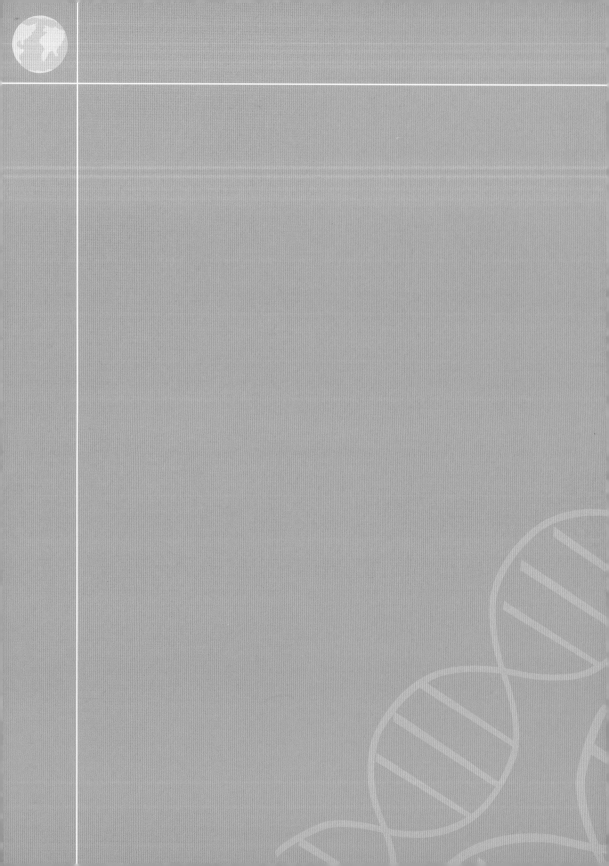

All About Mitosis and Meiosis

by Elizabeth R. Cregan

Science Contributor
Sally Ride Science
Science Consultants
Thomas R. Ciccone, Science Educator
Dr. Ronald Edwards, Science Educator

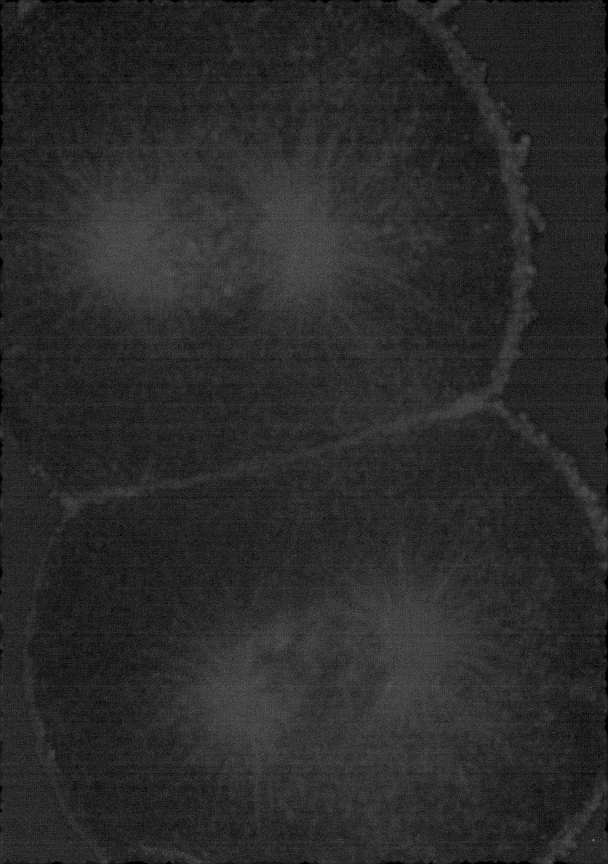

First hardcover edition published in 2010 by
Compass Point Books
151 Good Counsel Drive
P.O. Box 669
Mankato, MN 56002-0669

Editor: Mari Bolte
Designer: Heidi Thompson
Editorial Contributor: Jennifer VanVoorst
Media Researcher: Svetlana Zhurkin
Production Specialist: Jane Klenk

 This book was manufactured with paper containing at least 10 percent post-consumer waste.

Library of Congress Cataloging-in-Publication Data
Cregan, Elizabeth R.
 All about mitosis and meiosis / by Elizabeth R. Cregan.
      p. cm. — (Mission. Science)
 Includes index.
 ISBN 978-0-7565-4067-8 (library binding)
 1. Mitosis—Juvenile literature. 2. Meiosis—Juvenile literature.
 I. Title.
 QH705.C74 2010
 571.8'44—dc22   2009035401

Visit Compass Point Books, a Capstone imprint, on the Internet at *www.compasspointbooks.com*
or e-mail your request to *custserv@compasspointbooks.com*

Table of Contents

What Are Cells?

All living things are made of cells. A cell is the smallest unit of life. Some living things are a single cell. An amoeba, for example, is just one cell. Bacteria are single-celled, too. But some organisms are multicellular. That means they are made of many cells. Humans are multicellular. So are animals and plants.

Multicellular things can be made of trillions of cells. The larger the organism, the more cells it has. Cells have specialized jobs. They work together to help the organism do many things. They help it eat to create energy. They help it to get rid of waste. They even help it to reproduce—to make new cells.

◄ Each petal of each flower is made of hundreds of thousands of cells.

Mitosis and meiosis are the two processes by which cells reproduce. Plants and animals contain both body cells and sex cells. They reproduce in different ways for different reasons. Body cells reproduce to replace old cells or promote growth. This is asexual reproduction—mitosis. Sex cells reproduce to create new life. This sexual reproduction is called meiosis. But in order to understand these processes, we must first understand more about cells and how they work.

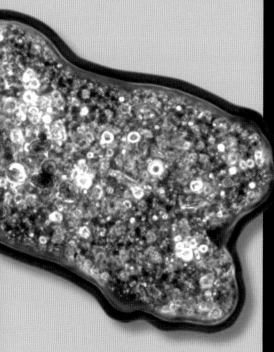

▲ An amoeba is a single-celled animal.

Take A Closer Look

The human body is made of 60 trillion to 100 trillion cells. About 25 million new cells are created each second. Most of these cells are very tiny. About 10,000 of them can fit on the head of a pin! But the sciatic nerve, which runs from the base of the spine to the tips of the toes, is more than 3 feet (1 meter) long.

Did You Know?

The nerve cells in a giraffe's neck can be more than 9 feet (2.7 m) long.

Cells are very busy. To work together, they must communicate with one another. They do this by exchanging chemical messages. The chemical messages move molecules from place to place. When your cells get a chemical message, they get busy. Thousands of these reactions take place in your body every second.

How Do Cells Know?

Have you ever cut your finger? Did new skin form?

Skin cells undergo mitosis to create new skin. Exact copies of skin cells are made to replace the ones destroyed by the cut. Growing new cells in this way may be called cell division. It is also known as asexual reproduction.

But how do living things create offspring? How do all the cells that work together to make one living thing get reproduced? Meiosis takes care of that. Meiosis is used in sexual reproduction. It is the process living things undergo to reproduce.

Robert Hooke
(1635—1703)

English scientist Robert Hooke was the first person to see a cell. In 1665, while observing a thin slice of cork under a microscope, he saw tiny boxlike shapes surrounded by walls. The walls and boxes reminded him of the tiny rooms that monks lived in, so he named the shapes after them: cells.

Plant and Animal Cells

Plant cells and animal cells are alike in many ways. For example, all cells are filled with cytoplasm, a fluid that contains everything the cell needs to live. The cytoplasm is contained by the cell membrane, which allows certain substances to pass through into the cell while keeping others out.

Both plant and animal cells also contain organelles. These are structures in the cytoplasm that perform certain jobs for the cell. Each one has a specialized role to play. Some turn food into energy, while others store water.

Did You Know?

In 1675 a scientist named Anton van Leeuwenhoek became the first person to describe red blood cells.

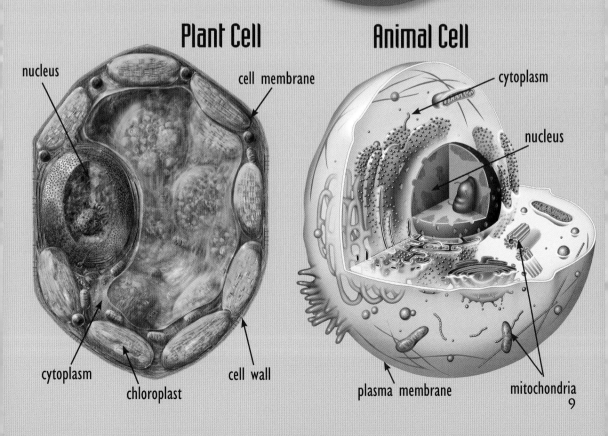

Plant Cell

nucleus

cell membrane

cytoplasm

chloroplast

cell wall

Animal Cell

cytoplasm

nucleus

plasma membrane

mitochondria

The cell's nucleus is inside the cytoplasm, too. The nucleus serves as the cell's control center. It also contains chromosomes, threadlike structures that carry genes. The genes are the basic unit of heredity. Together they make up a unique recipe for building a living thing. Genes are made of a chemical called

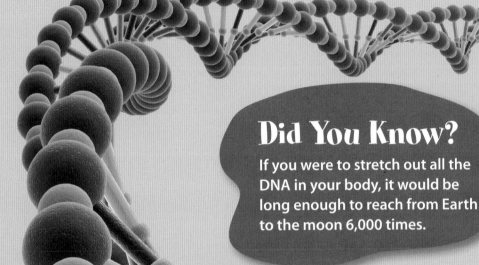

Did You Know?

If you were to stretch out all the DNA in your body, it would be long enough to reach from Earth to the moon 6,000 times.

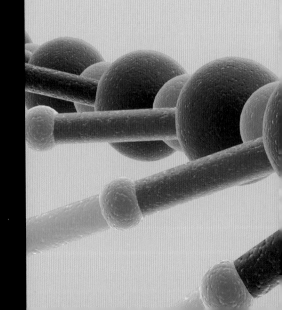

What's the Difference?

Plant and animal cells are different in some ways. Plant cells have a tough cell wall outside the cell membrane. They have less cytoplasm than animal cells do. Their organelles take up most of the space in the cell. Plant cells use organelles called chloroplasts to turn sunlight into energy. In animal cells, cytoplasm makes up half the cell. Organelles in the cytoplasm called mitochondria change the food animals eat into energy for the cell.

deoxyribonucleic acid. This is the substance that makes up our genetic code. A gene is a section of DNA that gives a specific instruction to the cell.

DNA is a long, stringy molecule that resembles a twisty ladder. Instructions along the string, called alleles, tell the cell when to make certain proteins. These proteins determine what the cell is like and what it can do.

◄ DNA has been called the blueprint of life.

There are two alleles for every gene. The cell follows both sets of instructions at the same time. It may make a lot of one protein if both alleles tell it to. Or it might make some of one protein and some of another if the alleles disagree.

Did You Know?

No two people but identical twins have exactly the same genetic makeup. You share 50 percent of your DNA with your parents and siblings.

DNA CSI

Because people have unique genes, DNA can be used to help solve crimes. Scientists can figure out a person's DNA fingerprint. They can then match the DNA to evidence found at the scene of a crime.

A person's DNA fingerprint is the same no matter what part of the body it comes

from. DNA can be found in body waste such as blood, semen, urine, feces, mucus, perspiration, and saliva. It is also found in skin and brain cells, body tissue, organs, muscle, bone, teeth, and hair. There is no known way to alter one's DNA, making DNA fingerprinting an important crime-solving tool.

What Is Mitosis?

Cells work hard. When they get old or damaged, they need to be replaced. Some cells are replaced frequently. For example, the cells in your stomach may only last a few days before the stomach acid destroys them. Others are almost never replaced. The cells in your brain are rarely replaced.

New cells also need to be created in order for a living thing to grow. Whether they are being created for replacement or growth, new cells are made through a process called mitosis. It is also known as cell division. The term comes from the Greek word *mitos*, which means thread. Chromosomes look like thread when cells divide.

Walther Flemming (1843–1905)

German scientist Walther Flemming was interested in cell division and chromosomes. In 1879 he discovered a threadlike material in the nucleus of cells. He also saw that the threads, now known to be chromosomes, shortened and divided during cell division. In 1882 he published a book, *Cell Substance, Nucleus, and Cell Division*, that illustrated and described the process of cell division. He called this process mitosis.

There are six stages to mitosis: interphase, prophase, metaphase, anaphase, telophase, and cytokinesis. Mitosis starts with one cell and ends with two.

Interphase

Most of the time, a cell is in a state called interphase. This is the time between cell divisions. A cell is in interphase 90 percent of the time. During this period, the cell prepares for mitosis.

Cells cannot just split in half. They create copies of themselves. The copies include their DNA.

interphase

Remember, the DNA is a blueprint for building new cells. The cell must be copied exactly. That is the only way each cell can survive and work properly. The duplication of a cell's DNA takes place during interphase. Now the cell is ready to divide.

Making Copies

The length of time required for a cell to make a copy of itself depends on the kind of organism and cell type. A sea urchin cell takes about two hours to duplicate, while a human liver cell takes about 22 hours.

Did You Know?

It takes between 12 and 24 hours for mammal cells to complete interphase. The rest of the mitosis process takes much less time— usually only one or two hours.

Prophase

During prophase the membrane that surrounds the cell's nucleus disappears first. Then the strands of DNA that paired off during interphase thicken. They become short, stubby rods called chromatids. They are attached at the center by the centromere. If you were to look at them under a light microscope, you would see that the chromatids look like the letter X. These tiny Xs become chromosomes. They contain the cell's genes—its genetic recipe.

cell during prophase

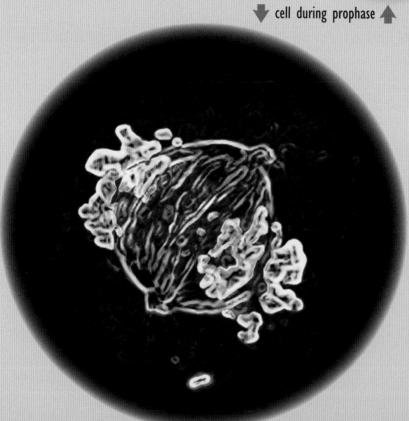

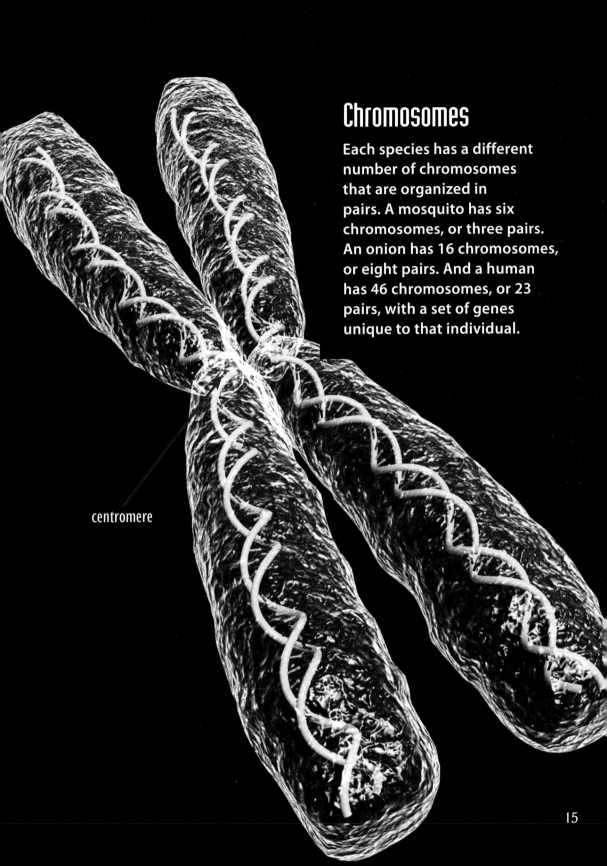

Chromosomes

Each species has a different number of chromosomes that are organized in pairs. A mosquito has six chromosomes, or three pairs. An onion has 16 chromosomes, or eight pairs. And a human has 46 chromosomes, or 23 pairs, with a set of genes unique to that individual.

centromere

Metaphase

The next phase of mitosis is metaphase. A chemical message tells the chromosome pairs to move to the center of the cell. The center is called the equator. The pairs follow orders and line up along the equator.

Structures called centrioles are located in the cell's north and south poles. The centrioles use protein threads to connect to the chromatids lined up along the equator. Each centromere becomes attached to one spindle fiber from each centriole pair. This connection is called a spindle. The cell is now ready to divide.

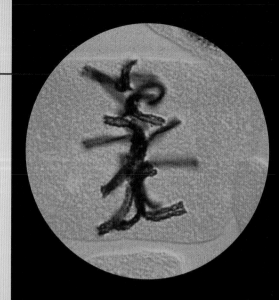

Take a Closer Look

The spindle fibers make sure each pair of chromosomes is lined up along the cell's equator. The spindle works to pull the chromosomes apart. Each new nucleus will get one copy of each chromosome. The threadlike structures in the image above are the chromosomes of a bluebell plant lining up during metaphase.

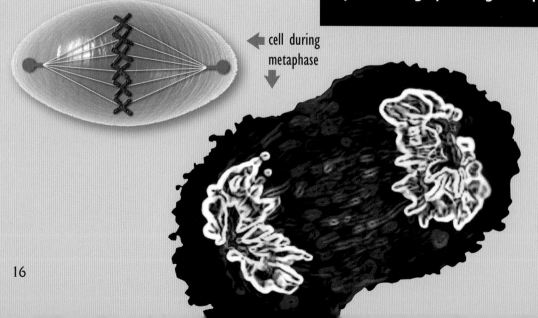

cell during metaphase

Anaphase

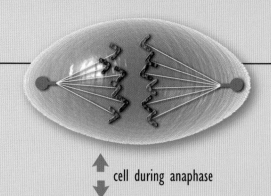

cell during anaphase

During anaphase, the cell signals the protein threads of the spindle to lengthen. This makes the cell longer, too. The threads pull the chromosomes toward the poles. The centromere divides, and the separated chromatids become independent chromosomes. Identical sets of chromosomes move toward the poles. Each pole now contains a complete set of chromosomes. When the cell divides, each new cell will contain a complete set of the same genetic blueprints.

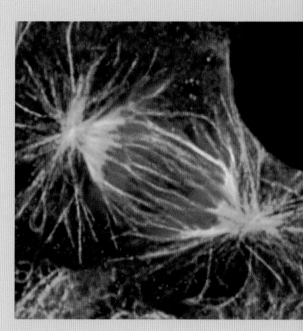

Sign of Mitosis

Have you ever seen a new shoot poking out of the soil in springtime? That is the result of mitosis. Has your sunburned skin ever peeled? The new skin that grows back is also the result of mitosis.

Telophase

Mitosis is nearly complete during telophase. The chromosomes finally arrive at the north and south poles of the cell. They begin to organize themselves into new nuclei. They are no longer visible under the light microscope. A membrane forms around each new nucleus. The spindle fibers begin to disappear.

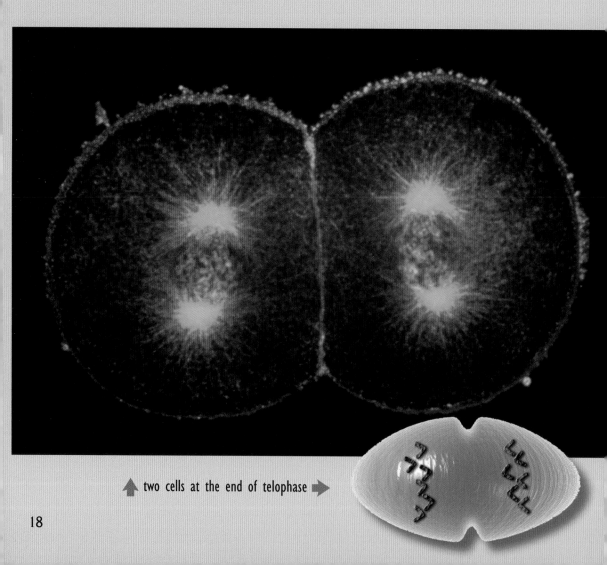

▲ two cells at the end of telophase ➤

Amazing Nature

There are substances in nature that can dissolve a spindle before it can pull the chromosomes to a cell's poles. Scientists know about two flowering plants that produce these substances. They are the autumn crocus and the Madagascar periwinkle. They stop cell division and growth. They are used to treat cancer and other diseases.

autumn crocus

The Name Game

When scientists discover a gene, they can name it whatever they want. That is why many have such interesting names. Did you know there is a hedgehog gene? There is even a T-shirt gene. One gene is called dreadlocks. What name would you pick if you discovered a gene?

Cytokinesis

Finally a dent or furrow forms down the center of the cell. In animal cells, this dent is caused by a fiber ring made of a protein. The protein is called actin. The ring pinches the cell into two identical cells known as daughter cells. In plant cells, a cell plate forms down the center of the cell. The cell breaks apart along

⬆ cytokinesis

the cell plate. This forms two daughter cells.

Nearly all cells go through mitosis. It helps repair and replace cells. It helps an organism grow. But it is not the only way that cells divide.

⬇ Both daughter cells contain the same number and quality of chromosomes.

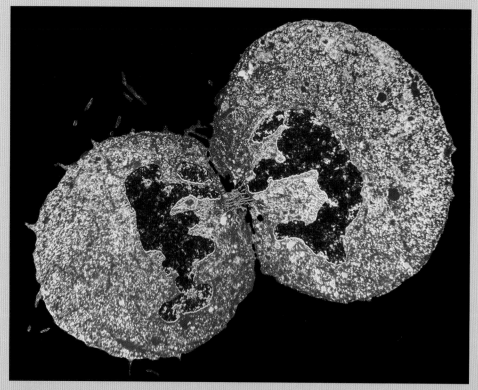

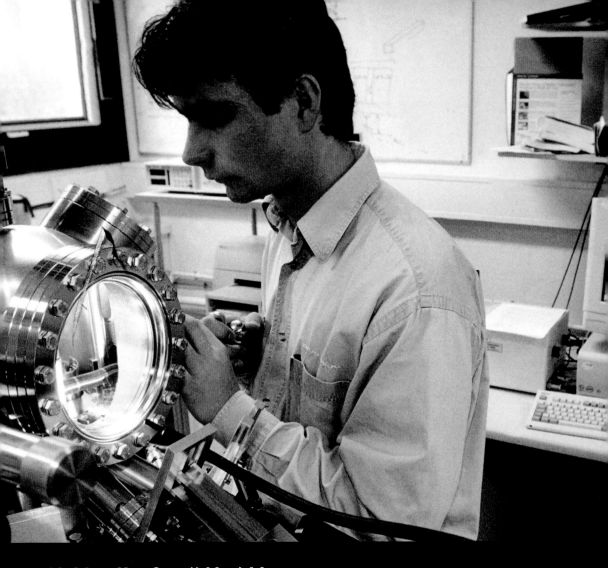

Making the Small World Larger

Light microscopes magnify specimens up to 1,000 times their size. They use a series of lenses to do this. The lenses focus the light that reflects off a specimen, which magnifies the image that we see.

One set of lenses focuses light on the specimen being examined. Another lens gathers the light from through a narrow tube. The tube ends in the third lens, the eyepiece. It then magnifies the reflected image.

Electron microscopes use electrons instead of light. They use a magnetic field as a lens. It focuses and magnifies the image of a specimen. Electron microscopes can magnify objects 2 million times.

What Is Meiosis?

Meiosis is the division of special kinds of cells. It is also called sexual reproduction. Unlike mitosis, meiosis produces four cells. These cells are called gametes. Instead of being identical to the parent cell, as in mitosis, in meiosis each daughter cell contains half the DNA from the parent cell. You can think of gametes as half-cells.

Many organisms—both plants and animals—have cells that undergo meiosis. Meiosis makes egg cells in human females and sperm cells in males. Flowering plants undergo meiosis. It makes megaspore cells in the flower's ovaries—the flower's female organ. It makes microspore cells in the stamen—the male organ.

Did You Know?

During meiosis, chromosomes can sometimes get mixed up and recombine in a variety of new ways. These new combinations give a wide range of genetic possibilities for the offspring.

How It's Made

Many plants and some animals are able to reproduce asexually. This means that there is only one parent.

For example, in jellyfish, corals, and some parasites, offspring develop as a growth on the parent's body and split off when they reach the right size. Certain worms split into several sections, each section developing into a mature worm. Some types of fish, insects, and

reptiles can produce eggs that don't require fertilization.

Asexual reproduction occurs much more quickly and uses less energy than sexual reproduction. It also allows populations to grow when there are few members. However, since it produces an exact replica of the parent, sudden environmental changes can mean extinction to anything that cannot adapt.

August Weismann [1834–1914]

August Weismann was a German scientist. He studied cell division of sex cells. He was the first to realize it had to be different from mitosis. He called this special division of sex cells "reduction division."

How Many Chromosomes?

Mitosis creates new cells. In humans, each cell contains all 46 chromosomes. Meiosis creates cells, too. But each cell has only 23 chromosomes. Two sex cells can join together and create a new organism that will have a new set of 46 chromosomes that no one has ever had before.

Genetic Mistakes

Cell division doesn't always work perfectly. Sometimes errors occur. Copying errors during cell division can produce a mutated cell. Mutations can also result from exposure to viruses, chemicals, or radiation. Sometimes mutations are helpful to a plant or animal, and sometimes they have no effect at all. Often, however, they are harmful. Some mutations result in offspring that have genetic disorders. Some children end up with too many chromosomes, and others have too few. Down syndrome is a genetic disorder in which people have an extra chromosome in one of the chromosome pairs.

Meiosis happens in two stages, called meiosis I and meiosis II. Both stages look a lot like mitosis. At the end of meiosis I, the original cell has split into two cells. Both cells have DNA, but not all of it. Each cell has two copies of half the original DNA. Later, meiosis II will split the two full cells into four half-cell gametes. Each gamete has one copy of half the original DNA.

Meiosis I and II each has four stages. They are prophase, metaphase, anaphase, and telophase.

They are numbered to match meiosis I and II.

Before meiosis I begins, the cell is in interphase. During interphase, the chromosomes and organelles are copied. The cell grows. Two pairs of centrioles appear in the cytoplasm.

Prophase I

Meiosis I starts with prophase I. The centrioles arrange themselves at the north and south poles of the cell. Strands

Alphabet Meiosis

One way to think of meiosis is using letters to stand in for the alleles being copied. The original cell might have alleles A, a, B, b, C, c, D, and d. Before meiosis, the genes are copied so the list becomes AAaaBBbbCCccDDdd. Meiosis I ends with one cell having AABBCCDD and the other cell having aabbccdd. Then Meiosis II splits those cells. The AABBCCDD cell splits into ABCD and

ABCD. The aabbccdd cell splits into abcd and abcd.

Of course meiosis I doesn't pay attention to which allele goes where. It could just as easily create cells with AAbbCCDD and aaBBccdd. They would split to two AbCD cells and two aBcd cells. Each cell would have one of each gene.

of protein shoot out from the centrioles. They begin to form the spindles. The nuclear membrane disappears. The chromosomes shorten and thicken. The spindles grab the chromosomes.

Chromosomes get in line on each side of the equator. Half the chromosomes are on one side and half on the other. The chromosomes stay with their copies. The spindle fibers shorten. They pull the chromosomes toward the poles of the cell.

Metaphase I

Metaphase I is the next stage of meiosis I.

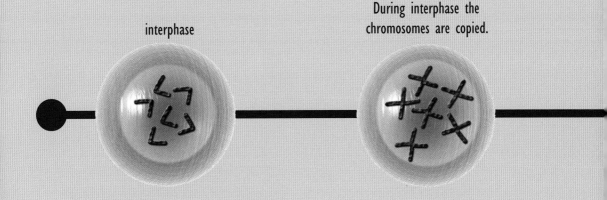

interphase

During interphase the chromosomes are copied.

During prophase I, centrioles reach out for chromosomes.

During metaphase I, the chromosomes separate into two complete sets.

Anaphase I

The third stage is anaphase I. The spindle fibers continue to shorten. The chromosomes are pulled to the poles of the cell. Because the chromosomes stick with their copies, each side has two copies of half the set. The chromosomes begin to organize themselves into new nuclei.

Telophase I

The process is completed during the last stage. A membrane forms around each new nucleus. A furrow begins to form down the center of the cell. The cell finally splits into two daughter cells. Each contains two copies of half the original DNA.

Twins

Identical twins are an interesting phenomenon. They are the result of both sexual and asexual reproduction. To create identical twins, a female egg is first fertilized sexually by a male sperm. Then the fertilized cell divides asexually by mitosis. Now there are two cells, called embryos. These embryos grow into two babies that contain the same genetic makeup. They are identical twins.

Did You Know?

In the United States, the average mother has a one in 32 chance of having twins. Nigerian women have the highest odds of twins—a one in 22 chance.

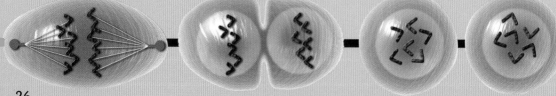

During anaphase I, the complete sets of chromosomes are pulled toward the centrioles.

During telophase I, the cell divides into two daughter cells.

During cytokinesis the cells rest.

The first stage is over. The original cell has split into two daughter cells. Each cell contains two copies of half the set of chromosomes. The cells rest. This is called interkinesis. It is different from interphase because the chromosomes are not copied. Then the cells begin to divide again.

Prophase II

New centrioles form in both daughter cells. They reach out to grab the chromosomes.

Metaphase II

The chromosomes are pulled toward the centrioles. Each centriole only pulls one copy of each chromosome.

Alternation of Generations

Sexual reproduction happens in many organisms. In many kinds of plants, it follows a two-step process. It is called the alternation of generations. The plant does the first half of meiosis to make a spore. It contains half the total number of chromosomes found in the rest of the plant's cells. The spores fall off and grow into a prothallus—a structure that contains the plant's sexual organs. It looks very different. The prothallus then does the rest of meiosis to make sex cells, which grow into a new plant.

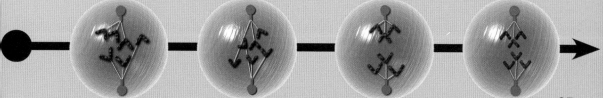

In prophase II, new centrioles reach out for chromosomes.

During metaphase II, the chromosomes separate into half sets.

Anaphase II

The chromosomes pulled to the centrioles get organized. They form into little clumps. Each clump has one copy of half a complete set of chromosomes.

Telophase II

A new nuclear membrane forms around the clumps of chromosomes. Each daughter cell splits into two new cells. Meiosis II ends with the creation of four daughter cells. Each one has half a copy of the original DNA.

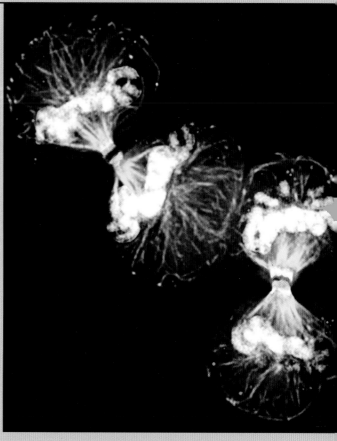

▲ Two cells during telophase II

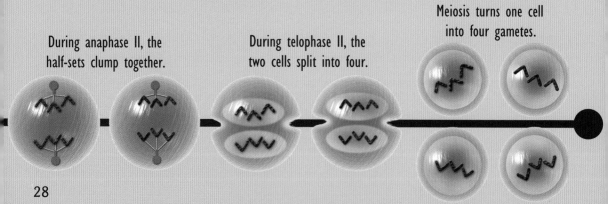

During anaphase II, the half-sets clump together.

During telophase II, the two cells split into four.

Meiosis turns one cell into four gametes.

What good are gametes with only half a set of DNA? In animals, a female's gametes are egg cells. A male's gametes are sperm cells. When an egg cell and a sperm cell are combined, together they have a whole set of DNA. The set has some chromosomes from the father and some from the mother.

The new cell uses mitosis to split into two cells. They become four, which become eight. Over time the cells can grow into a whole new organism. It will have some traits from its father and other traits from its mother. It will be their child.

Mitosis and meiosis work together and depend on one another. Mitosis helps living things grow new cells and repair damaged cells within themselves. Meiosis helps them produce whole new organisms that are their offspring.

Cell Model Mobiles

In this activity, you will make mobile models of plant and animal cells. Common household materials will be used to represent the structures of plant and animal cells. You will identify and describe the structure and function of organelles.

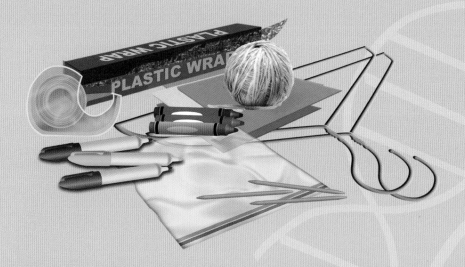

Materials

- construction paper

- crayons or markers

- tape

- wire clothes hangers (2)

- string or yarn

- plastic wrap

- toothpicks

- self-sealing sandwich bag

- notebook paper

- pen or pencil

Procedure

1 Use construction paper, crayons, and tape to make the following animal cell structures: nucleus, smooth endoplasmic reticulum, rough reticulum, mitochondria, vacuole, and lysosome.

2 Attach the animal cell structures to one of the clothes hangers, using the string or yarn.

3 Wrap the entire model in plastic wrap to represent the cell membrane.

4 Carefully insert toothpicks into the plastic wrap to represent cilia.

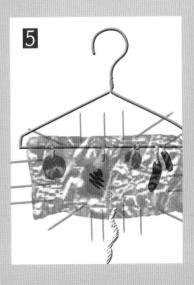

5 Attach a long piece of string or yarn to the plastic wrap or clothes hanger to represent a flagellum.

6 Use construction paper, crayons, and tape to make the following plant cell structures: nucleus, smooth endoplasmic reticulum, rough endoplasmic reticulum, mitochondria, chloroplast, vacuole, and lysosome.

7 Attach the cell structures to the second clothes hanger, using the string or yarn.

8 Wrap the entire model in plastic wrap to represent the cell membrane.

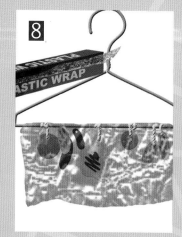

9 Cover the plastic wrap with the self-sealing sandwich bag to represent the cell wall.

10 On a sheet of notebook paper, list all the parts of the cells used in the cell models. Describe the design of your cell parts. The descriptions should explain how your cell parts work together.

Important People in Cell Biology

Walther Flemming (1843–1905)
German biologist who investigated cell division and how chromosomes distribute to the second nucleus; called process mitosis

Rosalind Franklin (1920–1958)
English scientist who made significant contributions to understanding the structure of DNA

Robert Hooke (1635–1703)
English scientist credited with observing the first cells under a microscope and naming the cellulae (cells); drew detailed images of his observations using a microscope and published them in 1665 in his book *Micrographia*

Anton van Leeuwenhoek (1632–1723)
Dutch scientist who made hundreds of microscopes and observed bacteria cells for the first time; commonly known as the father of microbiology

Karl Nägeli (1817–1891)
Swiss botanist who studied plant cells and used a special stain to see chromosomes better under a microscope; credited with observing cell growth and division

Walter Sutton (1877–1916)
American scientist who developed the chromosome theory of inheritance, which stated that both parents pass chromosomes to their offspring

James Watson (1928–   ), **Francis Crick** (1916–2004), and **Maurice Wilkins** (1916–2004)
Scientists from the United States, Great Britain, and New Zealand, respectively, who were jointly awarded the 1962 Nobel Prize in medicine for their discovery of the double-helix structure of DNA

August Weismann (1834–1914)
German scientist who was the first to realize that the cell division of sex cells was different from that of body cells; called this special division of sex cells "reduction division"

33

actin—protein that forms at the end of telophase; pinches the animal cells into two daughter cells

allele—one of two genes in a pair contributed by the parent

alternation of generations—two-step process of sexual reproduction in the life cycle of plants

amoeba—single-celled organism

anaphase—phase of cell division in which the spindle fibers shorten to pull chromosomes to the poles of the cell

asexual reproduction—form of reproduction that does not involve meiosis, gamete formation, or fertilization

centriole—structure that appears during metaphase that acts as the starting point for the protein strands that form the spindle

centromere—spot joining copied strands of DNA

chemical messages—how cells communicate and molecules move from place to place

chloroplasts—chlorophyll-containing organelle

chromatid—copy of a chromosome; occur in pairs after DNA replication, prior to mitosis or meiosis

chromosome—threadlike structure in the nucleus that carries the genes

cytokinesis—final phase of cell division in which the original cell is split to form two new cells

cytoplasm—fluid part of the cell where all cell functions are carried out

daughter cell—either of the two identical cells that form when a cell divides

DNA (deoxyribonucleic acid)—molecule of which genes are made

gamete—cell connected with sexual reproduction

gene—basic unit of heredity

interkinesis—the abbreviated interphase that occurs between meiosis I and II

interphase—period of cell growth

megaspore—larger of two types of spores that give rise to a female gametophyte

meiosis—two-stage cell division that produces sex cells with one set of chromosomes each

metaphase—phase of cell division in which the chromosome pairs move to the equator of the cell

microspore—smaller of two types of spores that give rise to a male gametophyte

mitochondria—organelles in a cell that convert energy from one chemical form to another

mitosis—cell division process that creates two new, identical cells

molecules—small bits of matter made of two or more atoms bonded together

nucleus—command center of the cell that gives instructions to the other parts of the cell

organelle—specialized part of a cell that has one or more specific functions

plasma membrane—membrane surrounding the cytoplasm of animal cells

prophase—first phase of mitosis in which the chromosomes appear

sexual reproduction—reproduction involving the union or fusion of a male and a female gamete

spindle fibers—tiny fibers seen in cell division

telophase—phase of cell division in which a membrane forms around each new nucleus, the spindle fiber begins to disappear, and a furrow begins to form down the center of the cell

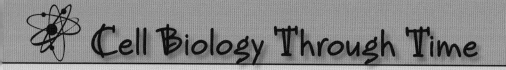
1665	English scientist Robert Hooke views the cell structure of cork under a microscope
1683	Dutch scientist Anton van Leeuwenhoek discovers bacteria cells by studying tooth plaque
1838	German botanist Matthias Schleiden finds that plants are made up of cells
1839	German scientist Theodor Schwann discovers protective cells on nerve extensions; he calls them Schwann cells
1844	Swiss botanist Karl Nägeli sees the process of cell growth and division under a microscope
1855	German doctor Rudolf Virchow states that all living cells come from other living cells
1882	German biologist Walther Flemming publishes a book that illustrates and describes cell division
1890	German biologist August Weismann discovers the importance of meiosis for reproduction and inheritance
1903	American scientist Walter Sutton determines that chromosomes may be the carriers of inherited characteristics; develops the chromosome theory of inheritance
1921	American scientist Thomas Hunt Morgan develops the idea that chromosomes carry genes, forming the basis of the modern science of genetics

1951	English scientist Rosalind Franklin begins using X-rays to study the structure of DNA
1953	DNA structure is discovered by American scientist James Watson and British scientist Francis Crick; their work is based on the work of Rosalind Franklin; English scientist Hans Adolf Krebs receives the Nobel Prize for his research on how energy is produced in cells (the Krebs cycle)
1954	Scientists discover that humans have 46 chromosomes
1986	Mammals—a cow and a sheep—are cloned for the first time
2003	The Human Genome Project is completed; 99 percent of DNA is sequenced
2006	American biologist Elaine Fuchs receives the Dickson Prize in medicine for her pioneering research on reverse genetics
2008	Researchers at Penn State University create an artificial cell in order to study the functions of the cell membrane and cytoplasm
2009	Scientists locate and modify mouse genes in order to understand how certain genes contribute to disease in humans

Johnson, Lori. *Cell Function and Specialization*. Chicago: Raintree, 2009.

Keyser, Amber. *The Basics of Cell Life With Max Axiom, Super Scientist*. Mankato, Minn.: Capstone Press, 2010.

Stille, Darlene R. *Animal Cells: Smallest Units of Life*. Minneapolis: Compass Point Books, 2006.

Stille, Darlene R. *Plant Cells: The Building Blocks of Plants*. Minneapolis: Compass Point Books, 2006.

Internet Sites

FactHound offers a safe, fun way to find Internet sites related to this book. All of the sites on FactHound have been researched by our staff.

Here's all you do:

Visit *www.facthound.com*

FactHound will fetch the best sites for you!

Elizabeth R. Cregan

Elizabeth Cregan is a freelance writer living in Jamestown, Rhode Island. She enjoys writing about a wide variety of topics for children and young adults including science, natural history, current events, and biography. She has a bachelor's degree in special education and a master's degree in distance education. She is also the owner of Cregan Associates, a consulting firm specializing in grant and technical writing for state government human services information technology clients.

Image Credits